First American Edition 2001 by Kane/Miller Book Publishers
Brooklyn, New York & La Jolla, California

Originally published in Japan under the title *Shippo no Hataraki* (*How Animals' Tails Work*) by Fukuinkan Shoten, Publishers Inc., Tokyo, 1969

Library of Congress Card Number: 00-109387

Printed and bound in Singapore by Tien Wah Press Pte., Ltd.
1 2 3 4 5 6 7 8 9 10

Animal Tails

by Ken Kawata
illustrated by Masayuki Yabuuchi
Yoshinori Imaizumi, Consultant

A CURIOUS NELL BOOK

KM Kane/Miller Book Publishers
Brooklyn, New York & La Jolla, California

This is a Spider monkey.
He uses his tail like an
extra hand.

He can pick fruit with it,
or use it to swing from
branch to branch.
It is a very useful tail.

This tail is short and stubby
and sticks straight up in the air!

Whose tail is it?

It's a Japanese monkey's tail!
Japanese monkeys live in big
groups called troops.

When one monkey wants to
let the others know that he
is tough and strong, he puts
his tail straight up in the air.

This tail swishes back and forth.
Whose tail is it?

It's a dog's tail!

Dogs use their tails to let others know how they feel. When they are happy, they wag their tails from side to side. When they are frightened, they tuck their tails between their hind legs.

This very long tail has
silky hairs on the end.
It's being used to chase
flies away.

Whose tail is it?

It's a cow's tail!
She's using it like
a fly swatter.

This fluffy tail is moving very
fast through the trees.

Whose tail is it?

It's a squirrel's tail!
He moves it back
and forth for balance.
When he jumps from
a tree, he uses his tail
like a parachute so he
won't get hurt.

This tail is long and very thick.
Whose tail is it?

It's a kangaroo's tail!
Her tail works like a cane
to support her body.
When she hops very fast,
she moves her tail up and
down for balance.

This long and bushy tail works
like a rudder for steering.

Whose tail is it?

It's a red fox's tail!
He's chasing after his prey!
When he's running, he moves his tail
sharply from one side to another to
change direction.

Here's a hint: this is not a fish's tail.
(A fish's tail stands straight up and down.)
Whose tail is it?

It's a dolphin's tail!
He moves his tail up and down
to swim through the water.
He can even jump out of the
water by snapping his tail down.

This tail is rattling and
telling others to beware.
Animals hurry away when
they hear this warning signal.

Whose tail is it?

It's a rattlesnake's tail!
He's poisonous! Keep away!

This tail is covered with spines called quills.

The raccoon got too close!

He got stuck! Ouch!

Whose tail is it?

It's a porcupine's tail!
His tail protects him from
other animals.

A chicken pecked this tail and it came off!
It's still wiggling!

Whose tail WAS it?

It was a skink lizard's tail!

His tail comes off very easily to help him escape from his enemies. Later, a new tail will grow in its place. What an unusual tail!

We have seen many different kinds of tails
that work in many different ways.
　　What other kinds of tails can you think of?
　　Do you know how they work?